LORI - Keep up the

[signature]

1

THIRSTY FISH

Darrell Scott
Joy Concepts
2018

FOR MORE BOOKS BY DARRELL SCOTT
www.dscottbooks.com
or
amazon.com/author/darrellscott

Dedicated to my wife, Sandy, and
to our children and their families

FORWARD by ERIN GRUWELL

At the heart of humanity is empathy - a desire to understand, to feel, and to see the world from another's perspective. Humans want to feel. We want to share and to find a place to put our emotions on display so that our pain, our love, and our joy can live forever in the hearts and minds of our friends, family, and anyone else who will listen. For my students, it was important to turn their pain into purpose and write what needed to be written.

When I first met the group of kids who would become my Freedom Writer family, many of them faced the threat of gun violence on the streets of their community. Too many of my students told me they have been to "more funerals than birthday parties."

It was hard to imagine a world in which students could endure such loss, such pain, and such horror before even graduating high school. The weight of these emotions, the stories of sacrifice and of suffering, would forever shape the lives of my students.

I hoped that by sharing their stories, my students could take these life changing events and change the world for the better. With pens in hand, my students took the name of "Freedom Writers" and turned to prose and poetry to prove that words, not weapons, would leave the most important legacy.

In the spring of 1999, the Freedom Writers were energized and optimistic about what the future held for them. Fresh from graduating high school the year prior, the Freedom Writers were in the midst of editing their book, *The Freedom Writers Diary*, and preparing for a trip to Europe to visit Anne Frank's attic and pay homage to the teen author who inspired their literary journey.

Then tragedy struck. The Freedom Writers and I huddled around a television and wept with fear and horror as we watched the atrocities unfold at Columbine High School.

While many of my students living in a gang-riddled community where violence was sadly all too common, what happened in Littleton was different. The Freedom Writers had grown used to dodging bullets on the tough streets of Long Beach, but they had always thought of school as being safe from this senseless violence.

It seemed impossible that Littleton, Colorado, a "safe" suburban community, could suddenly become a place filled with violence and fear as well. The atrocities at Columbine turned their understanding of "safety" upside down. Was no child safe? How does one make sense of the senseless?

While we were off to seek answers from Holocaust survivors abroad, we now knew there would be survivors of a different sort back at home. As we prepared for our trip to Europe, we decided we would light a candle for both Anne Frank and Rachel Scott alike to pay homage to innocent children everywhere who had lost their lives to hate and senseless violence.

All throughout our visit to Auschwitz, I thought about the heinous teen perpetrators in Littleton and their hateful killing spree at an idyllic high school. As we looked upon the evidence of pure evil at the concentration camp, I became more and more enraged, having heard the stories that the killers were brazen enough to do "Heil Hitler" signs in public view while bystanders stood by and did nothing.

Our guide through the camp, a Holocaust survivor himself, reflected my thoughts when he stated that "evil prevails when good people do nothing." As we departed Europe and returned home, we all were desperate to find good people doing something.

Luckily, upon our return to the states, we discovered that Darrell Scott was indeed doing something. As a father who had experienced inexplicable loss, he had turned his pain into purpose—poetry--and with his words, had become an accidental activist.

In honor of his daughter, Rachel, who like Anne Frank sought refuge with words, Darrell became an advocate in order to make sense of her tragic loss. Like Otto Frank before him shared his daughter's message with the masses, so too would Darrell carry on a legacy that was bigger than himself. Ultimately, words would prevail.

"Deep within me, loves replace
All the anger and the fear
In the stillness is a knowing
Who I am and why I'm here"
(From Darrell's poem: In The Quiet)

Since then, Darrell and I have become trusted friends and kindred spirits, and both believe the power that words bring. Through the years, I have shared his poetry with my students and teachers alike, because his words inspire the artist in all of us. Darrell's poetry is provocative and probing. It asks questions that linger and last. At times whimsical, others quite serious, reminding us that, "…awareness is the key, that liberates our anxious mind, and sets our spirit free."

As a teacher, I ask my students to study scholars who inspire them to hone their own voice, and now Darrell's poems are a part of their lexicon. Be it his description of a butterfly struggling to get out of its cocoon or even a crocodile who cries real tears, his metaphors have meaning. While my syllabus for English class includes Shakespeare and his sonnets, my syllabus for life now includes Scott's words of wonder.

In the moments of darkness, Darrell's poems bring us into the light. He reminds us of the Golden Rule, by embracing empathy, compassion and kindness. He leads with love, and his poetry is a reflection of such purpose. And thus, his poetic life's mission is a mandate that words matter.

"Now sticks and stones can make you sore
But words can hurt you even more
The things we say become so real
They either hurt – or help us heal."
(From Darrell's poem: The Fox, the Ox, and the Crocodile)

Poet's words, like Darrell's, stay with you long after the last stanza or you turn the page. His words sing and make your spirit soar. But most importantly, he encourages you to write. May Darrell Scott's profound poems encourage you, too, to become an activist. And may you, too, find that words, not weapons can heal hearts. As Darrell so eloquently shares in "Truth's Paradox":

"So keep an open heart and mind
For deeper truths are yours to find."

Erin Gruwell
Teacher, Author, Freedom Writers Founder

PREFACE

Poetry, art, and music are languages of spirit. They speak in a profound mystical voice that bypasses the methodical thinking of the brain, resonating with the truth hidden within us.

Whether the poet is Shakespeare or Dr. Seuss, their words strike a chord that remains in our memory - - often resurrected in moments of insight, tragedy, despair, or even levity.

Good poetry condenses volumes of research and data into a handful of words that have an impact on us in a way that facts, and figures, never can.

The poems in this book are creations that simply downloaded through me onto the pages. Often they came in complete form with no editing done on my part. Some are more "anointed" than others, but that may depend on their impact on the reader.

Poetry comes in all forms: freestyle, rap, rhyming, etc. All of my poems were written with meter and rhyme. There is no best way for poetry to be imparted. Sometimes meaning can be lost when the poet insists on rhyming. I have always admired those who can impart rhyming truth without losing its essence.

So I wrote this little poem to illustrate:

POEMS
darrell scott

A poem that rhymes, is really neat
A poem with meaning's, quite a feat
But poems with meaning, when they rhyme
Are poems that really are sublime!

My desire is that my "poetry with purpose" will inspire
you, and draw out of you the treasures hidden within!

LIFE LESSONS

PREFACE

1
IN THE QUIET
darrell scott

In the quiet, I find peace
Where the outside noises cease

When my mind has settled down
And my thoughts no longer race
In the chambers of my spirit
I have found a secret place

There the unseen things embrace us
The invisible that's real
And we there enjoy the treasures
That activity would steal

Hear the whisper of the poets
Who have beckoned us to know
Of that inner sanctuary
Where we seldom ever go

In the quiet of our being
Creativity is born
And it rises to the surface
To a world that's hurt and torn

Deep within me, love replaces
All the anger and the fear
In the stillness is a knowing
Who I am and why I'm here

2
MONKEY SALVATION
darrell scott

A monkey with a tender heart
Observed a fish in water
The monkey thought, "That stupid fish,
He really should be smarter"

The monkey snatched it from the lake
And placed it on the ground
He said, "You're lucky I was here
Or else you would have drowned"

The fish just flopped around a while
Until it finally died
The monkey sadly shed a tear
And said, "Oh well, I tried!"

We often think what's good for us
Is good for others too
But harm may come when we impose
Our biased point of view

3
NO WHIPPED CREAM
darrell scott

He stood at the counter, a smile on his face
And looked at the pictures in turn
The numerous flavors, and toppings, and nuts
But price was his biggest concern

"How much is a sundae with whipped cream on top"?
The little boy asked, being nice
The waitress was busy and hastily said
"A buck eighty five is the price"

She watched as he frowned and then slowly looked down
And counted the change in his hand
"So what would it be with the whipped cream left off?"
He nervously asked her again

"Look son, I am busy, and here is the deal
Without the whipped cream, it is less
A dollar and fifty five cents is the cost"
The boy's face reflected distress

He stood there, just thinking a moment or two
"Okay, I've decided" he said
"Well, what will it be?" she impatiently asked
And flipped back the hair on her head

"I'll take it without the whipped cream" he replied
"I think that is all I can pay"
She brought him the sundae, without the whipped cream
He ate it and then walked away

The waitress walked over to where he had sat
And cried as she chewed on her lip
That boy didn't order whipped cream, so that he
Could leave her a thirty cent tip!

4
SACRED SHOWER
darrell scott

The shower is my sacred place
Where water cascades down my face
And yielding to its warm embrace
My anxious thoughts can cease

And slowly I begin to see
The being that is really me
Immersed beneath this liquid sea
A presence full of peace

My thoughts now lose their strength and force
And yielding to a deeper source
They recognize a better course
Where only presence goes

Awareness now replaces thought
And mental battles I have fought
I realize were all for naught
As presence slowly grows

I find that "being" supersedes
My racing thoughts and active deeds
Replacing all my outer needs
With inward gentle power

Amazingly, this healing grace
Is always there for my embrace
And can be found at anyplace
Not just inside the shower

5
THE ROAD UNTRAVELED
darrell scott

I traveled down the broadest road
Where masses choose to go
I found it safe - - - but boring
Methodical and slow

It's well worn tracks and markers
All guiding me ahead
Where lifeless travelers move along
Like crowds of walking dead

But then I found another path
Less traveled than the rest
Not safe - - - but more exciting
A challenging new quest

And then one day I realized
That there was even more
A place beyond "less traveled"
Where none had yet explored

Excitement raced inside my veins
And purpose filled my heart
There were no footprints up ahead
Where I would have to start

I knew without a single doubt
This path was just for me
With faith - - and fear, I took a step
Toward my destiny

I saw and heard things yet untold
And moved in realms unknown
Down paths of risk and treasure
Where no one had ever gone

The road less traveled - - though it's grand
My friend, cannot compare
To one intended just for you
When purpose calls you there

Be not afraid to take that step
That leads to destiny
For only the untraveled road
Will set your spirit free!

6
MEMORY LANES AND FUTURE PATHS
darrell scott

Memory lanes and future paths, steal my thoughts away
Sounding so romantic, but distracting from today
Endless past that lies behind with laughter, pain and tears
Winding road that lies ahead with anxious hopes and fears

Past and future, thieves of now, causing me to see
Not what is, but what has been, and what is soon to be
Playgrounds of a restless mind, thoughts that never cease
Past and future tantalize, but never bring me peace

"Oh if only", "How I wish", deep regret and yearning
Always seeking after truth, but somehow never learning
Searching past and future for identity and pride
While the answer waits for us, hidden deep inside

Not aware of present things that often I would miss
By dwelling in a memory, or in thoughts of future bliss
Letting go of both I find, such beauty HERE and NOW
Living in Awareness as each moment shows me how

7
CHAMPIONS
darrell scott

You were one of many millions
Striving for a single goal
The first act of your existence
To become a living soul

From the start you were a winner
Although millions did compete
Only you would have a future
While the rest would know defeat

So the spark of life united
Through an intimate embrace
And another mighty champion
Now had joined the human race

There's a purpose to your being
There's a call to destiny
You were skillfully created
To be all you're meant to be

So when life seems disappointing
And you're tempted to lose heart
You can look back and remember
"I'm a champion from the start"!

8
DARE I LET MY DRAWBRIDGE DOWN?
darrell scott

Words, like arrows, pierced my soul
Meant to tear me down
Jokes and insults, snide remarks
Flying all around

Hiding in my castle walls
Feeling isolated
Like a prisoner locked away
Lonely and deflated

Texting, gossip, cyber pain
Catapults I fear
Flung from unexpected places
When no one is near

So I raise my drawbridge up
High above the moat
While I'm striving deep inside
To try and stay afloat

And then I see you once again
Arriving at my castle
Both of us with hurt and pain
So weary from life's hassle

So dare I open up again?
And dare I venture out?
And dare I let go of my pain?
My fearfulness and doubt?

I yearn to leave these walls of stone
But all of that depends
On whether I can trust once more
My family and my friends

So can you help me find the way
That leads to stable ground?
And dare I trust, yet once again
To let my drawbridge down?

9
A QUIET PLACE MY KINGDOM IS
Sir Edward Dyer: Reworded by Darrell Scott

A quiet place, my kingdom is,
And there such pleasures I do find
That far surpass the outward things,
That try to captivate my mind
I've learned to live without the things,
Desired by royalty and kings

No wealth, no fads that soon will fade,
No risky game that brings a thrill
No shiny toys, no fancy clothes,
They all will slowly lose appeal
And as my thoughts begin to cease,
I find a place of perfect peace

I see the wealthy unfulfilled,
And hasty climbers often fall
And those who choose to act so proud,
become the biggest fools of all
They gain by toil, they keep by fear,
Their smile devoid of any cheer

I find contentment is my goal,
While others wallow in their greed
I realize that outward things,
Can never meet my deepest need
I now live inward like a king,
Content with what awareness brings

Some have too much and crave for more,
A hunger that will never end
I have not much, but live in peace,
Content with what I have within
They're poor, I'm rich, They beg, I give,
They slowly die, I daily live

I laugh not at another's loss,
I envy not another's gain
For I'm connected to the source,
And live in peace that few attain
I fear no foe, I flatter none,
And I will live 'till life is done

Some find their pleasure through their lust,
While others rule by stubborn will
In gold and silver is their trust,
While some seek purpose through a thrill
But all the treasure that I find,
Is found beneath a quiet mind

My health and ease are all I need,
A conscience clear of all deceit
No bribe nor threat to taint my deed,
An honest pathway for my feet
It's how I live, it's how I'll die,
I wish that all could do as I

10
TAKE NO THOUGHT
darrell scott

The Teacher taught to "Take no thought"
I thought of what he said
What did he mean to take no thought?
He's messing with my head

I analyzed his every word
My thoughts were racing 'round
I sought for deeper meaning
And I searched for higher ground

Exhausted and frustrated
I eventually let go
Of trying hard to understand
This truth that I should know

And then my mind just settled down
And peace that I had sought
Came flooding in - - the moment when
I chose to have no thought

11
DARKNESS FIGHTER
darrell scott

I cursed the darkness all night long
It wouldn't go away,
I threatened, yelled, and pleaded
But the dark was here to stay

I held an anti-darkness sign
But no one there could read it
It seemed that there was just no way
The dark could be defeated

I formed a Darkness Fighter's Club
To rid us of the plight
And many came, with hearts aflame
To purge the dark of night

We voted and we passed a bill
An anti-darkness law
We chanted at a rally
'till our vocal chords were raw

We mocked it and we called it names
We created a scandal
'till someone handed me a match
And helped me light a candle

Then suddenly the darkness fled
The room just came alive
Don't fight the night, just shine a light
And darkness can't survive!

12
WISDOM REPLIES
darrell scott

A wise man sat on the edge of town
When a stranger traveled by
"What kind of folks will I find here?"
He asked with a heavy sigh

The wise man answered, "How were folks
In cities where you've been?"
"They're crude and rude, with attitude"
The stranger said; and then

The wise man slowly cleared his throat
And said, "It's sad, but true
The people here will be the same
As all those places too"

Another stranger passed his way
And in a little while
He asked the same old question
But he asked it with a smile

The wise man answered, "How were folks
In places where you've gone?"
"They're kind and happy" He replied
"They'll treat you like their own"

The wise man slowly smiled and said
"My friend, you'll find it's true
That people here will be the same
As all those places too"

13
I DIDN'T KNOW I KNEW
darrell scott

When I was young and full of self,
A wise man said to me
"Someday your eyes will open, son,
Someday you'll come to see

That down beneath your ego,
Endless wisdom does abide
And all you ever need to know,
Is hidden down inside"

I thought the man was crazy,
And I laughed at what he said
He smiled and gently added,
"But it's not inside your head"

The years have flown and I have grown,
My ego left behind
A "knowing" has awakened,
From my spirit, not my mind

I'm more than just the thoughts I think,
I AM - - and that is why
In stillness I have come to know,
The Source is my supply

I understand what that old man,
Once spoke is fully true
From inward flow I've come to know,
I didn't know I knew!

14
FORM & FORMLESS
darrell scott

A beautiful mansion of classic design
A structure that all could admire
"But where did it come from?" I thought to myself
And so I set out to inquire

The homeowner told me the house started out
As blueprints designed by a friend
An architect labored to lay out a plan
Expressed by his paper and pen

I asked where the blueprints and plan had come from
He smiled and replied, "From my head.
My thoughts turned to paper, then blueprints, and then
The house was completed" he said.

So what birthed the thoughts that expressed as a house?
The questions went deeper, of course
The thoughts came from somewhere and as I pressed on
I entered the ultimate source!

Exploring the place where the wonder set in
A place only spirit can see
A place that transcended the visible realm
Where substance and form cease to be

The mansion, the blueprints, the plan, and the thoughts
Were all different forms of expression
Emerging from formless, invisible source
That ultimate place of perfection

15
THE BROOK AND THE BOULDER
darrell scott

A massive stone yelled at a brook
"I'm here to wear you down"
The brook just rippled 'round the stone
And hardly made a sound

The years flew by, the decades passed
The brook began to grow
It covered up that mighty stone
Its trickle, now a flow

Today the rushing waters roar
The sound will make you quiver
That stone is now a pebble
At the bottom of the river

16
THE CALM PSALM
darrell scott

The poet wrote, "I shall not want"
I thought, "How can that be?"
That one could live a life fulfilled
Not wanting what they see

But soon I learned that all those things
Could never quite fulfill
The longing that I felt within
For something that is real

I sought the mystery in its forms
But then I failed, of course
For joy and peace could not be found
Except within the Source

The shadow cannot satisfy
It only leaves us bound
Until we yield to stillness
Where the substance can be found

Once found, the Source provides us
With the things to be enjoyed
But when the things control us
Then our peace will be destroyed

The poet wrote, "I shall not want"
And I too have agreed
That things can never satisfy
The Source is what we need

17
FAKER
darrell scott

I think that you are very fake
You artificial flower
It's true your leaves will not soon fade
It's true, you need no shower

But can you duplicate that smell
Of what you imitate
Or can your leaves turn golden brown
As winter brings your fate

Will bees come buzzing all around
To pollinate your plant
Will you provide the nectar
For the honey? No – you can't!

You have a great appearance
But so sadly, you're a faker
It seems to me that you reflect
The talents of your maker

18
BEAUTY and UGLY
darrell scott

Beauty and Ugly went out for a swim
They put all their clothes on a low hanging limb

Soon Ugly climbed out (he was ready for bed)
He reached for his clothes but grabbed Beauty's instead

When Beauty got out, she had nothing to wear
So she grabbed Ugly's clothes that were still hanging there

Now Beauty is hidden by Ugly's disguise
And Ugly's attractive to gullible eyes

So Ugly gets praised, and poor Beauty abused
And too many times, people get them confused

'Cause Ugly looks good 'till he's fully exposed
And Beauty is often disguised by her clothes

But when you look closer, I think you'll agree
Most beauty is deeper than what you can see

19
BUILT or BUILT-IN?
darrell scott

Remember when we used a map
To help us find our way?
It showed us every road to take
And places we could stay

We'd take a pen - - sit down – and then
We'd slowly trace a route
So we would know, where we should go
Once we were headed out

Then one of us would hold it,
In our hand or in our lap
Until the driver turned to say,
"It's time to use the map"

We'd check the route and then call out
"Turn left around the bend"
And that's the way, we'd spend our day
Until the journey's end

And then the GPS appeared
To take us down the street
And we would find the folded map
To now be obsolete

A screen would show which way to go
And lead us all the way
A ladies voice would make the choice
And we would just obey

And I remember thinking,
Just how smart we really are
To go from maps to GPS
That helps direct our car

Until I heard, a flock of birds
As I sat down for dinner
Without a map or GPS
They flew straight south for winter

If we can learn to look inside,
When things all fall apart
We'll find that built-in GPS
Abiding in our heart

That quiet voice will guide our choice
As turbulence is stilled
From outer noise to inner poise
Our pathway is revealed

20
THE FOX, THE OX, AND THE CROCODILE
darrell scott

A fox, an ox, and a crocodile
All met to visit for a while
They each were sad, and shared their grief
Of being judged by wrong belief

The fox said, "Everyone I know
Says I am sly, and it's not so
It makes me feel, like I'm a sneak
When really, I am kind and meek

The ox then slowly cleared his throat
"You know what really get's my goat?"
The goat said, "Hey don't judge me man!"
(He'd just walked up and joined the clan)

The ox replied, "I'm sorry dude
It's just that people are so rude"
"He's dumber than an ox", they say
It hurts me – 'cause that's not okay

The Croc just nodded, and agreed
"You're right, it really hurts, indeed!
They say my tears are all just fake
And when I cry, that's hard to take!"

They shared how others judged them wrong
How words can hurt for oh, so long
They hugged and left – each with a smile
The fox, the ox, - - the crocodile

Now sticks and stones can make you sore
But words can hurt you even more
The things we say become so real
They either hurt – or help us heal!

21
SUFFERING IS OPTIONAL – PAIN IS NOT
darrell scott

A part of every human path
Includes some measurement of pain
The hurt is real and often deep,
And may result in loss or gain
But much depends on how I think,
That causes me to rise or sink

If I'm aware, detached from thought,
The pain will not control my life
But if I focus on the hurt,
I only create inward strife
The hurt will grow, and linger on,
And thrive beyond the pain alone

Most pain will come without my choice,
While suffering, I've come to find
Is but an option that I choose,
Through thoughts created by my mind
When thought is stilled, I found such peace,
That causes suffering to cease

So choose to lean toward the pain,
With no resistance from your mind
Detach from thought and be aware,
And soon my friend, you'll come to find
That peace replaces all our fears,
And suffering just disappears

22
THE WORD IS NOT THE THING
darrell scott

You can never get drunk from just saying "Wine"
You can never be full from just saying "Dine"

You can never get stung from just saying "sting"
'cause quoting the word doesn't make it the thing

You can talk about travel and places to roam
But you'll never get there just by sitting at home

To say that you own it is clearly absurd
If all you are doing is saying the word

23
THIRSTY FISH
darrell scott

Can you imagine thirsty fish?
Or one afraid to drown?
Or singers and musicians
Who are scared to make a sound?

And yet so many live in fear
Of what might come to be
Instead of living in the "now"
Enjoying liberty

Anxiety has bound their heart
Their eyes no longer shine
They live in prisons brought about
By thoughts within their mind

Detachment is the answer
And awareness is the key
That liberates our anxious mind
And sets our spirit free

24
THEY KNOW NOT WHAT THEY DO
darrell scott

The walking dead are everywhere
They know not who they are
They work all day, and sleep all night
They travel near and far

Unconscious of their "being"
Simply "doing" all day long
Dissatisfied and unfulfilled
Yet sensing something's wrong

So lost in thought they wander 'round
In circles of confusion
Obsessed with "things" that cannot break
Their prisons of illusion

The answer lies within them
But, they're blind and cannot see
The straight and narrow path that leads
To life and liberty

Until they can awaken
To the Source known by so few
Oh Father, please forgive them
For they know not what they do

25
FORGIVENESS
darrell scott

Such words of wisdom I have heard
That have a deep and truthful ring
From Ghandi and Mandela too
As well as Martin Luther King
The weak cannot forgive, they said
They cling to bitterness instead

Forgiveness is misunderstood
By those who hold to pain and rage
Their freedom gone, they choose to live
Like prisoners in a dreadful cage
They can't let go, they can't forgive
And so in bondage they now live

Forgive, and you can be set free
Your life will now move on ahead
No longer bound by things long past
Existing like the walking dead
Forgiveness opens up a door
That sets you free to live, once more

Unforgiveness keeps you chained
To those who chose to do you wrong
Always seeking for revenge
Silencing your inner song
Forgive and you will find release
Into a place of restful peace

26
DON'T HELP THE BUTTERFLY
darrell scott

One day I watched a butterfly
Emerge from its cocoon
It pushed and struggled mightily,
And then it seemed to swoon

Half in, half out it hung there,
And I began to doubt
That it would ever make it through
- - And so I helped it out

I took a pair of scissors,
And I slowly cut away
That all confining structure,
That had held it in its sway

But then I came to realize
The damage I had done
I watched the poor thing flounder
As it lay there in the sun

Its wings deformed and incomplete,
It made me want to cry
By helping I had sealed its fate,
It now would never fly

In sadness I stood watching
As it drew its final breath
By helping with the struggle
I had guaranteed its death

If only I had chosen
Not to lend a hand that day
If only someone had explained,
And I had walked away

That butterfly would now be free
To flap its wings and fly
To soar away throughout the day
Into the endless sky

I need the wisdom to discern
When I should lend a hand
Or sometimes, absolutely not,
I've come to understand

That struggle, sorrow, tears, and pain
May open up a door
That we alone, may come to own,
That place from which we soar!

27
SHADES OF SHAKESPEARE
darrell scott

The raven's wings may filthy be
Yet none will stare, or even see

But if upon the white dove's breast
The smallest speck of dirt should rest

The criticism would be heard
About this filthy little bird

Another's flaws we oft demean
So our own faults will not be seen

28
RENEW YOUR VIEW
darrell scott

A wise old man once said to me
"Don't trust the things your eyes can see
For if you do, you'll know confusion
Always judging by illusion

Don't look at - - see through my friend
Beyond the frown, the sneer, the grin
Peer deep into the living soul
Where beauty, wonders will unfold

Fear and judgment fall apart
When our view is from the heart
So don't look at, adjust your view
And focus deeper, seeing through

29
RITUAL or REALITY?
darrell scott

Baptized in water, I simply got wet
While none of my spiritual needs had been met

I tried to be better, I acted the part
I said the right words from my mind, not my heart

I worked and performed and I gave it my best
But knew in my heart that I failed every test

Frustrated and angry, I gave up - - and then
Awareness through stillness arose from within

The peace and the joy that had long been denied
Were there all along – simply hidden inside

Through yielding and stillness, true strength I did find
The treasure within me, a source so divine

Not might, nor can power force open the door
But stillness releases our spirits to soar

30
SEED THOUGHTS
darrell scott (adapted from a poem called: "The Critic")

A little seed fell in the ground beneath a massive tree
Someday, it mused, when I grow up, I wonder what I'll be
And so it lay there in the dirt, just dreaming in the gloom
And wondering what it would be when it began to bloom

It thought awhile and with a smile it analyzed the rose,
"It comes in different colors, and it's pretty I suppose,
But thorns are there and I declare, there seems to be a lot
So when it comes to roses, well, I think I'd rather not"

"The daisy seems quite happy as it wiggles in the grass
But yellow's not my color, so I think I'll let it pass
The lily is a noble plant, but just too white, you see
It's not the kind of flower I would really like to be"

It lay there in its bed of dirt and spent each passing hour
Just judging and eliminating each and every flower
And so it analyzed them all, this criticizing seed
Until it woke one summer day, a scraggly bitterweed!

31
WHEN "I AM" SAYS "Yes" TO THE "NOW"
darrell scott

I once tried to change, the things I distained
Frustrated – I didn't know how
Then deep from within, a thought did ascend
"Let 'I AM' say 'YES' to the NOW"

I've learned to let go – to merge with the flow
No longer by sweat of my brow
My struggles all cease, embracing the peace
When 'I AM' says 'YES' to the NOW

All war will dissolve, and peace will evolve
Such beauty this world will allow
Deep love we will see, and oneness will be
When 'I AM' says 'YES' to the NOW

DIVINE CO-INCIDENTS
darrell scott

Today we met, it seemed by chance,
(If you believe in such)
But what instead, if Cosmic plan
Designed our lives to touch?

A minute more, a minute less
A stop – a text – a call
A skip in time, and you and I
Would never meet at all

Some say its luck, or happenstance
Some say it makes no sense
But I embrace, the arms of Grace
Divine Co-Incidents

CHOOSE TO LOSE
darrell scott

Lose your mind and find your purpose
Let your frenzied thinking cease
Through detachment and surrender
You will find a lasting peace

Walk the small, constricted pathway
Into life you never knew
There emerging into purpose
Realized by just a few

Lose your mind and enter stillness
Where your purpose will unfold
There your spirit will awaken
Through a quiet, resting soul

Grace and purpose will surround you
And such treasure you will find
When you yield to God's intention
And you choose to lose your mind

34
THE STONE IN THE ROAD
darrell scott

Once upon a time long gone
Inside a path there stood a stone
And everyone would go around
That great big stone placed on the ground

Some traveled left and some veered right
And everybody felt uptight
'Cause going 'round it wasn't fun
especially in the summer sun

So people cursed the stone each day
Just wishing it would go away
It caused a problem for them all
Because the stone was wide and tall

But then one day a man came by
He saw the stone, and with a sigh
He pushed and rolled the stone away
Although it took the entire day

And when his task was finalized
He just could not believe his eyes
For lying in a great big hole
There sat a sparkling pot of gold

The man had done his kindly deed
To just help out, and fill a need
So unexpected – his reward
But it was placed there, with regard

Because the king had put it there
Just hoping that someone would dare
Remove the stone and by his action
Teach his kingdom true compassion

Not for money, not for fame
Not so folks will know our name
Acts of kindness, words of grace
Make the world a better place

35
REALIZATIONS
darrell scott
(inspired by a quote from my daughter, Rachel)

Realizations come to me
In unexpected ways
Things untold and things unseen
Emerging from the haze

Out of nothing they appear
And open up my eyes
And seeing the invisible
I've come to realize

That music is more beautiful
Than instruments reveal
And power is much greater than
The power lines can feel

The painter knows he limits
The expression of his art
The poet never can express
The message in her heart

While systems stifle all the life
And spontaneity
The Source that's hidden by the haze
It seems to beckon me

Spontaneous and risky
Are the places I'll pursue
But freedom there emerges
In a way known by so few

I've learned to see beyond my view
And I have come to find
That limitations don't exist
Except inside my mind

The things I see and things I feel
Are limited, of course
But I have learned to look beyond
I've come to trust the Source!

36
SPIRIT LANGUAGE
darrell scott

Appearance is the garment of the Spirit
Calling us to go behind the veil
Deep calls unto deep if we can hear it
Speaking things no human tongue can tell

Most will spend their lives and never live them
Tethered to the things that can't provide
Blinded to the Source that wants to give them
Everything they yearn for deep inside

Language of the Spirit can't be spoken
Yet, it whispers truth each night and day
Heard by only those who have been broken
Those who know the Truth, the Life, the Way

Appearance is the garment of the Spirit
Calling us to go behind the veil
Deep calls unto deep if we can hear it
Speaking things no human tongue can tell

37
THE HIDDEN
darrell scott

Much doctrine and teaching has hidden Your presence
Religion and dogma, distorting Your essence

You're sought by so many, and found by so few
You're easy to find if the seekers just knew

They go to a building with singing and prayer
They reach out to touch You and hope You are there

They visit Your presence, but fail to abide
They don't understand that You're always inside

They claim that they'll find You, whatever the cost
But they don't understand that You never were lost

Stop searching "out there", it's like chasing the wind
For That which you seek for is hidden within!

38
WHY THE BIRD SINGS
darrell scott

The bird never sings
Just to give a confession
The bird never sings
Just to teach us a lesson

The bird never sings
To enlighten our mind
With doctrine, or dogma,
Or teachings divine

The bird simply sings
Without motive or ploy
Expressing a heart
That is bursting with joy

39
THREE QUESTIONS
darrell scott

Two questions that were answered
Far before my time on earth
Who I am, and why I'm here,
Were known before my birth

That "knowing" was distorted,
And too soon I lost my way
My thinking mind had made me blind,
And filled me with dismay

I sought for answers everywhere,
But I was doomed to fail
Until my search turned inward
And I passed behind the veil

Into a place of peace and joy,
And truth that can't be taught
Awareness grew, and then I knew,
The answers I had sought

But those two answers weren't enough,
Somehow my spirit knew
That who I AM and why I'm here
Must lead to what I do

For being leads to doing,
And the doing must reveal
The deeper things that spirit brings
To help our planet heal

Too often we're content to "be",
Embracing inner rest
While all the while the Source intends
For us to manifest

The formless must express through form
For it to be complete
So from the heart, I must impart,
To everyone I meet

40
POSSUM OR OPOSSUM?
darrell scott

Is it possum or opossum?
That has always bothered me
I've been asking folks that question
Since the day that I turned three

Everybody gives an answer
But I never seem to get
An agreeable solution
'Cause it seems that folks are split

There's the 'possum' crowd from Texas
But the folks from Delaware
Just insist that its 'opossum'
It's confusing, I declare

How can one word be so tricky
I just really want to know
Do I start it with the letter 'P'
Or with the letter 'O'?

41
DIFFERENT PERSPECTIVES
darrell scott

Prisoners sitting in a cell
One in heaven, one in hell
One was looking at the bars
While one gazed out at twinkling stars

In a hospice two are dying
One is smiling, one is crying
One at peace, her conscience clear
One in turmoil, dread, and fear

Some feel hope and some despair
Some will bless and some will swear
Some feel whole and some defective
Each expressing their perspective

42
BREAKING THROUGH
darrell scott

In the turbulence of thinking
Peace and joy can never last
Only worry and frustration
Of the future and the past

False projections from an ego
We pretend we never had
While the fruit of our existence
Leaves us unfulfilled and sad

But the choice to enter stillness
Breaking ego's crusty shell
Opens us to realms of heaven
While escaping pits of hell

Deep beneath the noise of thinking
Is a river full of peace
In the stillness lies the answer
Causing ego's reign to cease

So, in stillness we awaken
Through awareness we explore
Peace and joy and such contentment
That we never knew before

43
THE SECRET WAITS
darrell scott

The Secret waits in silent poise,
While we are seeking 'round
Deep down inside it does abide,
Just waiting to be found

Both peace and joy evade our grasp,
Its fruit cannot be bought
The Secret will, in time reveal,
In stillness - - what we sought

44
THE WATCHER
darrell scott

Like sirens screaming through the streets
Like drummers pounding different beats
My thoughts are racing at a rapid pace

A joke, a story, doubt and fear
Thoughts so cloudy, thoughts so clear
They fill my mind like runners in a race

Thoughts build me up, thoughts tear me down
They jerk emotions all around
I'm drowning in a wild, chaotic sea

Some give me hope, and some despair
A lofty dream, a bad nightmare
And I have come to think that they are me

But slowly I became aware
Of Presence, sitting, waiting there
Behind the thoughts that never seem to cease

That Presence is the real me
And I have come to clearly see
That as the Watcher, I can live in peace

I'm not the thoughts I think each day
No longer guided by their sway
In stillness I observe their scam

The truth that's there for all to find
Is deeper than the thinking mind
The watcher is the person that I AM

45
KNOWERS SAYERS
darrell scott

I've heard that those who know, don't say
And those that say, don't know
I puzzled over this all day
A thought began to grow

I'll ask a Master who is wise
To help me understand
Why knowers seldom verbalize
But sayers always can

The master listened to my plea
And struck a thoughtful pose
He asked "Can you define for me"
The fragrance of a rose?"

My mind was racing for a while
And then I understood
And slowly I began to smile
Just like he knew I would

For beauty, fragrance, joy, and pain
A sight, a sound, a smell
Are things we sometimes can't explain
And words would simply fail

So, knowers are content to know
While sayers help us see
That constant chattering will show
How futile words can be

MUSINGS AND MEMORIES
darrell scott

Musings of the future,
Memories of the past
Products of a restless mind,
Thoughts that never last

Robbing us of Presence,
Stealing joy and peace
Like a storm tossed ocean
Full of waves that never cease

Past and future both the same,
Prisons of illusion
Flawed, elusive dwelling places,
Fostering confusion

"Has-been", "will-be" we are not,
We were meant to "be"
What can save us from our thoughts?
What can help us see?

Stillness is our teacher,
And Presence is our guide
Moving from a thinking world,
Toward a place inside

Saving us from fruitless thought,
Gently showing how
Teaching us Awareness as
We're living in "THE NOW"!

47
POGO'S WISDOM
darrell scott

Pogo told us long ago,
A truth that sets us free
For he unveiled a secret
That is sometimes hard to see

He calmly made a statement,
Without drama – without fuss
He said, "We've met the enemy,
the enemy, is us!

So when you point your finger
When you judge, or criticize
Remember Pogo's wisdom
And you soon will realize

The problem's not in others
Or from anything outside
The enemy is plain to see
Your ego and your pride

So when you choose to put away
Your false identity
And let unfold the YOU inside
You'll find that you are free

You'll break the chains of selfish need
Of pressure, and demanding
And live in realms of joy and peace,
That pass all understanding

48
KNOW-BE-DO
darrell scott

Once my life was full of "doing"
All the things that needed done
On the surface always busy
Working, playing, having fun

But a yearning deep within me
That I just could not ignore
Gently drew me from the shallows
Into waters far from shore

There I found a deeper purpose
And my heart was clearly seeing
That activity can hender
True expression of my "being"

Now my "doing" had a reason
And my "being" was fulfilled
But a voice within me whispered
"There are things yet unrevealed"

So I ventured ever deeper
Without effort, without force
To a realm of simply "knowing"
In the stillness of the source

Many spend their life just "doing"
And their "being" never soars
Through the deep and mystic waters
Far from noisy, cluttered shores

Some will come to find their "being"
Living free of guilt and fear
While a few embrace the "knowing"
Who they are - - and why they're here!

49
FELT or TELT?
darrell scott

It's better felt than telt
It's better touched and smelt
Than all the knowledge you acquire
Or doctrines you have helt

Experience, not knowledge
Awakens us within
So joy and peace can now increase
And purpose can ascend

Awareness opens fountains
That thinking never will
The streams abide, down deep inside
Until our mind is still

Awakening to purpose
Aware of here and now
With hearts aglow we start to grow
As spirit shows us how

It's better felt than telt
It's better touched and smelt
Than all the knowledge you acquire
Or doctrines you have helt

50
THE PURPOSE OF A SEED
darrell scott

What is your purpose, little seed?
What will you grow to be?
A pretty rose? A piece of grass?
A bush? A vine? A tree?

The seed replied, "I'd like to know
But I am in a jam
My shell must break and I must die
To find out who I am"

"If I refuse, I'll stay the same
My destiny untold
I'll never know until I yield
And let it all unfold"

And so the seed fell in the ground
And waited patiently
Until within, there did ascend
A giant Redwood tree

51
LEAVE THEM ALONE
darrell scott

Don't dig up the seed
To see if it grows
Don't pry at the bud
To make it a rose

These creatures of beauty
Mature on their own
So – do them a favor
And leave them alone!

Don't try to change others
Your spouse or your friend
You'll just create chaos
Again and again

Let change start within you
And quite soon you will see
That others will change
When you just let them be!

52
TRANSFORMED
darrell scott

One day I'm a winner, the next day, I'm down
I feel like a king, then, I feel like a clown

I'm feeling discouraged, and then feeling strong
My feelings revealing that something is wrong!

And so I ignored them, and turned to my head
My thoughts and ideas would lead me instead

However, again, I was tossed, all about
With wild speculations, theories, and doubt

And then I discovered, in stillness, the key
My thoughts and my feelings were lying to me

And now I am freed by the truth I embrace
I can't change myself - - but I'm transformed by grace!

53
BOOMERANG
darrell scott

"What goes around must come around"
A quote that we all know
And all of us have heard the phrase
"You reap just what you sow"

The more I give - both good and bad
Will oft return to me
In bigger portions than I gave
I've finally come to see

As karma circles back again
This lesson I have learned
When aiming fire at others
I'm the one that may get burned

My cutting words, my harmful deeds
Affect how others feel
And I have come to realize
That time will wound all heels!

54
DOCTRINE and DOGMA
darrell scott

The mind is locked, the heart is blocked
When doctrine rules the day
While creeds may kill, the spirit will
Reveal a better way

"It's either/or - - It's neither/nor
Says dogma to the head
But spirit to the heart replies
"Consider this instead - - "

A Word today, that shows the way
May soon become my jail
Imprisoning my future steps
And causing me to fail

The written law, does have a flaw
It's rigid, without grace
Let love prevail, and you can tell
When truth has found its place

55
MYSTIC PLACE
darrell scott

Facts and figures help explain
Through methodical design
Solid knowledge that we gain
As we memorize the line

Yet the methods that we learn
Cause a bondage deep within
And our hearts begin to yearn
For a pathway to ascend

Metaphoric sights and sounds
Lead us to a mystic place
Where the wonder still abounds
Limitations are erased

Art and poetry reveal
Myth and legend can unfold
Deeper truth that none can steal
From the chambers of our soul

Nameless realm of mystery
Where our spirit can be shown
Views that only heart can see
Unexplained - - yet fully known

56
TEACHER or MASTER?
darrell scott

The teacher explains
To enlighten your mind
With facts and with figures
And words that define

The master tells stories
That fully impart
Awareness of Source
That awakens your heart

The teacher instructs
So your knowledge will grow
The master imparts
Far beyond what you know

57
TRADE YOUR CLEVERNESS
darrell scott

When ego is controlling me
Illusion settles in
I only see the surface
Not the wealth that lies within

Enamored by appearances
Impressed by wealth and fame
While never understanding
That it's all a shallow game

But then I am awakened
And my blindness has been healed
And I embrace the treasures
That the Source has now revealed

I'll trade my fleeting passions
For the joys that never cease
My cleverness for wisdom
As awareness bring me peace

58
BLIND SEARCHERS
darrell scott

George rode his horse
At breakneck speed
While shouting
All through town

"I'm looking
For my horse
And he is
Nowhere to be found"

They laughed at George
And called him names
Like "idiot"
And "clod"

But I have heard
Of those who say
"I'm searching
For my God"

59
CONCEPTS
darrell scott

Concepts color comprehension
Creating illusion
Causing us to live a life
Of blindness and confusion

Letting go of our ideas
On how things ought to be
Awakened to the way things are
Allowing us to see

Preconceptions fall away
Anxiety will cease
Awareness rises from within
Providing lasting peace

60
HINDSIGHT – CONCEPTS – VISION
darrell scott

As I look back and learn
From all that hindsight has instilled
My concepts are empowered
By what history has revealed

The glasses that I see through
Now are tinted by my view
My dreams and my perceptions:
All I say, and think, and do

My vision and my heritage
Are rooted in my past
The things that really matter
And the deeds that tend to last

So concepts formed by hindsight
Are reflected in my vision
Entangled all together,
They affect today's decision!

61
HOST or HOSTAGE?
darrell scott

A hostage to my ego?
Or host to Source within?
The choice is mine and I will find
That what I choose will win

My ego will enslave me
While Source will set me free
Will boastful pride or peace inside
Dictate who I will be?

The path I choose determines
The substance or the scam
To chart my course, I yield to Source
Revealing who I AM

62
LIVING IN THE MOMENT
darrell scott

Depression, guilt, despair, and shame
Children of a cluttered mind
Focused on what's done and past
Dwelling on the things behind

Dreading what might come to be
Living in a future place
Tension, stress, and needless fear
Products of an anxious pace

Void of joy and lasting peace
That's available today
Missing beauty that somehow
Past and future stole away

Letting go of all the past
And what future things could be
Living in the moment now
As awareness sets us free

63
QUALIFICATION FOR PEACE
darrell scott

Oh mighty sage, great man of peace
Such wisdom you have spoken
How can my inner turmoil cease?
He said, "You must be broken"

Your gifts and talents, waste away
Where ego does abound
Humility must rule the day
Or peace will not be found

Resist and you will only know
Anxiety and pain
But let your inner being flow
And peace will always reign

Embrace the pace, and yield to grace
Just let your mind be stilled
With dignity, you'll find your place
And live a life fulfilled

64
THE BROOK AND THE OCEAN
darrell scott

I explained to a brook
Of the powerful ocean
Its thunderous waves
And magnificent motion

The brook thought a while
And then said with a smile
"You exaggerate friend,
That's a fictitious notion"

And then to the ocean,
I spoke of the brook
It waved me away
And it called me a crook

"You're lying" it said,
As it rolled on ahead
And left me behind
With a withering look

65
A SEED SUCCEEDS
darrell scott

A flower seed is small indeed
There's nothing much to see
It tumbles down – upon the ground
Beneath a shrub or tree

But deep inside – there does reside
A flower - - - unassuming
That in the spring, will do its thing
And slowly start a-blooming!

It first must lie there in the ground
Invisible awhile
Until the sun invites it out
And greets it with a smile

With culture right, and climate bright
That shell will slowly break
And life within, will now ascend
A flower will awake

Emerging slow, that plant will grow
And everybody knows
That from that seed, the life indeed
Will thrill us - - as a rose

66
A TEACHER'S CALLING*
darrell scott

We are not called to fill a pail
While others try - - and often fail
Our calling is to start a fire
Awakening a deep desire

Fueling hope and aspiration
Wonder, awe, and expectation
Learning then becomes alive
And not a task for which we strive

So light the blaze within their heart
And watch the education start
For they are not an empty pail
But vibrant fires that will prevail

(Inspired by a quote from William Butler Yeats:
"Education is not the filling of a pail,
but the lighting of a fire")

67
AIMLESS PATH
darrell scott

If you don't know where you're going
Any path will take you there
You will wander in the darkness
Of frustration and despair

In the quiet, learn to listen
You will find your proper course
In the stillness of your being
Hear the wisdom from the source

Books and teachers may assist you
Songs and prose may help you see
But they only serve as arrows
Pointing t'ward your destiny

Cancel all the noise and clamor
Hear the whisper of the wind
For the path to true fulfillment
Is the path that lies within

68
ALI-USION
darrell scott

She *seemed* to be a gentle soul,
The kindest in the crowd
While he *seemed* full of arrogance,
Belligerent and proud

She went to church each Sunday,
Where she graced the second row
While he was in the boxing ring,
Just pounding on his foe

She clasped her hands and closed her eyes,
And prayed a pious prayer
He scandalized the nation,
With his boasting and his flair

She made a great impression,
As a proper southern belle
While he defied the status quo,
And ended up in jail

But yet I saw a difference,
And I came to these conclusions
They both were contradictions,
On the surface - - just illusions

Beneath her kind demeanor,
Was an angry, judging soul
Religious and self-righteous,
No compassion, hard and cold

While he would scowl and taunt us,
With his fist held up so high
But quickly I had learned to see,
The twinkle in his eye

His arrogant demeanor,
Was a purposeful distraction
'Cause soon we came to know a man,
Of grace and deep compassion

Her life was all impressions
Full of surface implications
While his would leave a legacy,
That impacted the nations

Too often we are hoodwinked
By an action or a look
So never judge a cover,
"till, my friend, you've read the book!

69
AWAKEN
darrell scott

From awareness as an infant
Curiosity awakens
But the wonder soon will vanish
In a world of regulations

Rules and dogma, stats, opinions
By the letter, by the number
Lead to uninspired existence
In a life of routine slumber

Shed the darkness, light the candle
Let your spirit now ascend
May the child from deep within you
Reawaken once again

70
BRING YOUR "A" GAME
darrell scott

Be **AWARE**, if you dare
Of the things you cannot see
Through the eyes of mystic knowing
Viewing authenticity

Past the surface misconceptions
Through the feelings of confusion
You will find your core of meaning
Just beyond the Great Illusion

With your **ATTITUDE** adjusted
And your gratitude in place
You can take a course of **ACTION**
To impact the human race

Who you *are* is more important
Than the things you *say* or *do*
AUTHENTICITY emerges
To express the real you

71
CHILDREN OF YOUR "WHY"
darrell scott

Now performance is important
To accomplish any goal
And the process must be working
For the outcome to unfold

But the thing that's most important
Isn't "what" or "how" or "when"
It's the "why" behind the purpose
That ensures a fruitful end

For performance without purpose
Is a lifeless piece of art
And the process lacking passion
Is a system without heart

All accomplishments that matter
Come from spirit's vast supply
When your passion and your purpose
Are the children of your "why"!

72
DON'T JUDGE THE COVER
darrell scott

Too often we evaluate
Another human being
Because of what they wear or say
Or what we think we're seeing

We criticize the words they speak
And judge the things they do
And never seem to take the time
To hear their point of view

For if we did, then we might find
A person just like us
Someone that we could call a friend
Or even come to trust

That someone hidden by their skin
Deserves a deeper look
So please don't judge a cover friend
Until you've read the book

73
DUEL DISGUISES
darrell scott

Emerging from our common source
We started down this human course
Until illusion blocked our way
And ego taught us what to say

With words like "you" and "them" and "me"
We lost our true identity
And blinded by our selfish pride
We choked the peace we had inside

So separated from our source
We lived by cunning, wit, and force
Until we came to realize
The emptiness of our disguise

But through humility and grace
We traveled to that quiet place
Of peace, and love, and harmony
For all of us are one, you see

We ceased from treating others wrong
Our uni – verse became one – song
No longer seeing "her" or "him"
'Cause "they" are "us" disguised as "them"!

74
EGO'S SCAM
darrell scott

Believing that my thoughts are me
Has caused me such confusion
Creating false identity
Resulting in illusion

But yielding to a quiet mind
Exposing ego's scam
By letting go, I've come to know
In stillness - - who I AM

75
EMBRACE THE PACE
darrell scott

My life is totally complete
As I pursue my course
Embracing joy, as well as grief
Both coming from the source

Accepting, not resisting
Both the sunshine and the rain
Understanding in my heart
That growth must come with pain

I've learned that when I murmur
Or complain about my plight
I stifle the creative
And I cloud my vision's sight

Resistance only strengthens
That which I would view as wrong
The high - - and low notes, both are there
To help express my song

The more I fight, the less I win
I only bring delay
Ignoring all the lessons
That would help me on my way

So I embrace, with thankful heart
And to the source I yield
In faith that all that comes my way
Will form a life fulfilled

76
ET TU?
darrell scott

Last week in Mrs. Wilson's class
We learned of Julius Caesar,
The story was quite boring,
But I read it just to please her

It told about a man betrayed
By those who knew him well
They stabbed him in the back and then
He died, so goes the tale

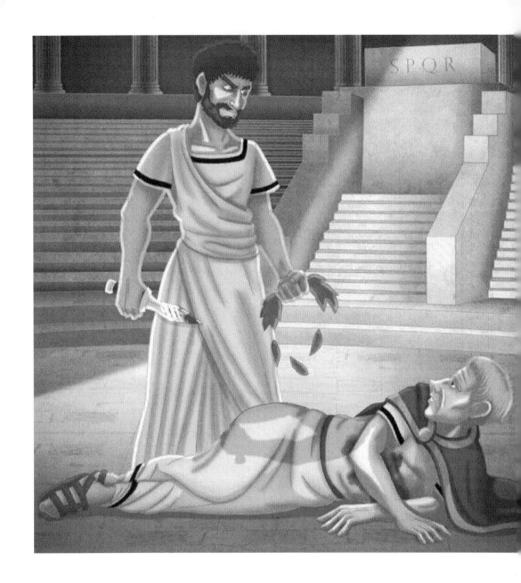

Now Marcus Brutus was a man
Who Caesar called his friend
But when the stabbing started,
There was Brutus joining in

And Caesar with his dying breath,
Would slowly turn his way
He looked at him with words so grim,
And said, "Et Tu Brute"?

The story didn't mean too much
Until today at school
When I was shoved and yelled at,
And was called a brainless fool

I thought that you and I were close,
But when they bullied me
You stood there just pretending
That you didn't even see

I thought that you and I were friends,
But when you saw my fear
You joined in with the others,
As you stood there with a sneer

And then I knew how Caeser felt
When Brutus stabbed him too
The words that hurt the deepest,
Were the ones that came from you

77
HIDE AND SEEK
darrell scott

Hide and Seek, a game from Source
Beckons us each day
Curiosity, of course
Makes us want to play

Looking here and looking there
Never satisfied
Oh if we would only dare
Find what's deep inside

Masquerading in disguise
'Neath mind's endless chatter
Treasure hidden from our eyes
Spirit clothed in Matter

Trying, giving it our best
Grasping at illusion
Tiring of the endless quest
Ending in confusion

Many never play the game
Some begin - - but cease
Sidetracked by their wealth, or fame
Never finding peace

78
I AM ESSENCE
darrell scott

I AM essence - - full completion
No addition, no depletion
Formless Being, here, eternal
Needing nothing of external

Temporarily expressing
Form that's rapidly digressing
Understanding, fully seeing
That the formless is my Being

All expression's just excess
Causing worry, and distress
Form, illusion, con, and sham
Lasting essence is: I AM

79
ILLUSION OR REALITY?
darrell scott

Though I'm a little overweight
My shadow's good to me
'Cause early in the morning hours
It's tall and thin, you see

It changes shapes throughout the day
This shadowy protrusion
But now and then, when it is thin
I love this kind illusion

My mirror on the other hand
Reveals reality
Reflecting just exactly what
I didn't want to see!

So do I want to know what's real?
Or do I choose the fake?
Illusion is the choice, I fear
That most will often take

So some will choose to fill their days
Surrounded by illusion
And then they wonder why they live
A life of such confusion!

80
INTERTWINED
darrell scott

There is no dawn, without the night
No victor's crown, without the fight
No birth can come, without the pain
No rainbows shine, without the rain

A perfect world without its flaws
Would need no purpose, goal, or cause
Each day the same, no noble quest
No good, no bad, no great, no best

The ups and downs, the ins and outs
The joy, the fear, the faith, the doubts
The form and formless, heart and mind
All deeply meshed, all intertwined

And so we walk this road of life
Embracing peace, as well as strife
Through hurt and joy, our hearts ascend
By dual paths of yang and yin

81
TEACHERS: LET IT UNFOLD
darrell scott

They're young, they're green, they're so uptight
There's so much they don't know
We want to help them do what's right
We want to help them grow

But we have learned without a doubt
That forcing them is wrong
We dare not strive to help them out
We cannot write their song

By love and patience, let them grow
And furnish what they need
Providing soil and water so
They finally do succeed

We cannot make them open up
We cannot play their role
But if we love and nourish them
Their purpose will unfold

The strain is real, the struggle hard
But everybody knows
With love and light, when time is right
That bud becomes a rose

82
LIQUID, VAPOR, ICE
darrell scott

Liquid, vapor, frozen ice
All from water came
Very much like you and I
Different, yet the same

Each revealed in varied ways
Each unique, of course
All expressing forms of life
Flowing from the Source

83
LISTEN
darrell scott

Have you ever shared your feelings
To a friend whose eyes were glazed
And you knew she wasn't listening
'Cause her mind was in a haze

She was waiting till you finished
Just ignoring every word
Unconcerned with your opinions
She just wanted to be heard

Let her rudeness be a lesson
Others think that you are smart
When they have your full attention
And you're listening from the heart

Just one mouth is all we're given
But two ears are also there
So it seems that we should listen
Twice as much as we should share

84
PERSPECTIVE
darrell scott

Turtles are so very fast
I don't know how they do it!
They seem to fly across the ground!
(That's how a snail would view it)

85
THE SEARCH
darrell scott

"Who am I?" I hear the cry
Though words are never spoken
A silent plea to know the "me"
Not false egoic token

The search is done by everyone
But many never find
They tend to cling to anything
That entertains the mind

When hope seems lost, some pay the cost
Their efforts finally cease
And letting go, they come to know
A lasting inner peace

It can't be bought by focused thought
By outward scheme nor scam
The real me, I've come to see
In Stillness is I AM

86
SOURCE OR EXPRESSION?
darrell scott

Your smile can sometimes make me sad
Your compliments can make me mad
The hidden source is much more real
Than what expression might reveal

Your words can seem like empty space
Your silence can impart such grace
The things I sense or things I see
Which ones can really impact me?

Your smile can hide the anger there
Your angry words may show you care
My life has taught me this conclusion
What I see - - may be illusion

It seems that I am most impressed
By unseen source, not what's expressed
The things I sense inside of me
Are much more real than what I see

SOUL AND SPIRIT
darrell scott

Soul and spirit aren't the same,
(As so many do declare)
Though they both remain invisible,
Big differences are there

One is Source and one expression,
One the thinker, one the thought
One eternal, one but fleeting,
One the teacher, one the taught

Mind, emotions, and volition,
All components of the soul
Meant as servants to the spirit,
As they each express their role

While the spirit's intuition
And communion with the Source
Has a conscience there to guide it
As it navigates its course

Soul and spirit, separated,
Meant to work in harmony
Bringing peace and joy and presence,
To a life that's been set free

With the power of a lion
And the meekness of a lamb
So aware, in quiet stillness,
The eternal, great I AM

88
ROBBERS
darrell scott

Past and future - - thieves that steal
What the present would reveal
Lost in memories, dreams, and goals
While ignoring what is real

Backward look and forward glance
Keep us bound within a trance
Stealing chapters of our lives
Unaware of present chance

Peace and joy are never found
When our search is outward bound
Both await from deep within
While we're seeking all around

Trading now for what will be
Or some bygone memory
Unaware of here and now
Blinded from reality

Spirit speaks through quieted mind
Oh what treasures there we'll find
When the stillness grips our soul
Peace and joy and love divine

89
REBORN
darrell scott

See the little caterpillar
Crawling down the street
Moving very slowly
At a dull and steady beat

It just takes forever
Going here and going there
Life for caterpillars
Is a heavy load to bear

"I'm viewed", she said, "By others
As a lowly little pest
I think that I will crawl away
And build myself a nest

So she went into hiding
And from others she withdrew
'Cause sometimes caterpillars are
A lot like me and you

But then she came out of her shell
And rose to greet the sky
Her crawling days are over now
'Cause she has learned to fly!

So when you're feeling down and out
By different little things
Remember caterpillars
And be sure to spread your wings!

90
OLD BOOKS
darrell scott

Their pages are tattered,
Their covers are dusty
They've yellowed with age
And they sometimes smell musty

They've served, oh so many,
And all through the years
They've challenged us, humored us,
Brought us to tears

Their authors are gone
But their words still inspire
They prompt us to action
And help us acquire

The wisdom of prophets,
The knowledge of ages
By reading their words,
We can all become sages!

But now they are threatened,
And I greatly fear
That if we're not careful,
They'll all disappear

The web has become
An incredible crook
It's stolen the pleasure
Of reading a book!

91
SNOW WHITE'S PRINTS
darrell scott

The dwarfs all bought a camera,
And they gave it to Snow White
She snapped a lot of pictures
All day long and through the night

But when she took them to the store
To have them printed out
The manager was sick that day,
He had a case of gout

She left them at the counter,
She was feeling pretty glum
Until the clerk assured her that
"Someday your prints will come"!

92
TRUTH'S PARADOX
darrell scott

The things that I believe today
Have guided me along my way
But what I think – and know so well
May soon become my prison cell

There was a time when wooden boats
Were all we built - - because "wood floats"
But deeper thinking would reveal
That better boats are made from steel

The VCR and corded phone
Are now a memory long since gone
The newest concepts we embrace
Will soon dissolve without a trace

So truth unfolds its many sides
As wisdom whispers and confides
And like a sly but crafty fox
Its voice may seem a paradox

The truth today that sets me free
Tomorrow, may imprison me
And so I've learned that what I know
May shift and change, to help me grow!

Pre-suppositions do abound
False premises are all around
So keep an open heart and mind
For deeper truths are yours to find

93
VOICES
darrell scott

A voice kept speaking in my head
It filled my mind with fear and dread
It drove me totally insane
Through endless movies in my brain

I longed for solace and relief
From tortured thoughts and wrong belief
Then slowly I began to find
That I could change my thoughts and mind

So I began to emphasize
The positive, instead of lies
But still the noise just never ceased
If anything, it just increased

I knew this endless flow of thought
Could never bring the peace I sought
It seemed that I would never find
Escape from such a restless mind

Then letting go I came to see
My thoughts were never really me
The secret that I've come to know
Is how to yield to present flow

Now released from thoughts control
I have found my place and role
Freed from living as a sham
Understanding who I AM

94
THERE GOES THE ROSE
darrell scott

If the petals told the prickly thorns
"You're ugly, dull and plain"
And if the thorns should answer back
"We're sharp, while you're just vain"

And if they both should tell the stem
"Your view is just too straight
You have no personality
So boredom is your fate"

And if the stem should tell the leaves
"You're always wearing green
You're using me to just hang out"
Now wouldn't that be mean?

And if the leaves should tell the roots
"You're stuck beneath the ground
Invisible, and useless
And you never make a sound"

And if their friendships fell apart
Then everybody knows
Their awful fight would seal their plight
And there would be - - no rose!

95
THE WORST THING
darrell scott
(from a quote from Bob Mumford, my lifetime mentor)

The only thing worse than a critic
Is a friend who would fill you with flatter

The only thing worse than a failure
Is succeeding at things that don't matter

96
FORREST or YODA?
darrell scott

Forrest Gump just walked around
He lived without a plan
No anxious thoughts could hold him down
This simple, peaceful man

While Yoda learned to live beyond
A frenzied anxious mind
From stillness he could now respond
With wisdom unconfined

So rise above the realm of thought
Let frenzied thinking cease
Embrace the wisdom you have sought
And live a life of peace

97
CLEVER or WISE?
darrell scott

I listened to a clever man
His mind was sharp, his words were grand
His gifted tongue knew what to say
To hold a crowd within his sway

But then I heard a wise man speak
His tone was mild, his spirit meek
His words brought healing to my heart
And gave my life a brand new start

So if my choice were "smart or wise"
It should not be a great surprise
While cleverness may have its place
It's wisdom that I would embrace

98
QUIT PEEING
darrell scott

Both **p**seudo and **p**sychic begin with a "**P**"
Pso why **p**shouldn't **p**sofa or **p**sandles or **p**see?

And why isn't **p**numbers just **p**spelled like **p**neumatic
(I'm **p**sure I must **p**sound like a **p**eeing fanatic)

Psadness, **p**sea-**p**sickness, **p**supper, and **p**seize
They all **p**should begin with those unspoken "**P**"s

Pso here's what I'm thinking and what I've been **p**seeing
We must change our **p**spelling and **p**stop all that "Peeing"!

99
PITY THOSE GUYS
darrell scott
(Adapted and amplified from another short poem)

Pity those guys who analyze
Who sit around and ostracize,
And demonize, and criticize
Those guys they envy and despise,

For they will have a great surprise
When they begin to realize
That all the guys they demonized
Begin to rise above the guys
Who sat around and criticized

100
AN APPLE SEED
darrell scott

An apple seed will never birth
A tangerine, or dog
It will not birth a grizzly bear
An apricot, or hog

An apple cannot be a plum
And orange you glad for that?
For there would be confusion
If an eagle birthed a cat

A seed can only reproduce
The fruit from which it came
So apple seeds birth apples
And the cycle stays the same

101
ENEMIES OF PEACE
darrell scott

Two foes that rob us of our peace
Without them, all our troubles cease
The first – desire, the second – fear
Remove them - - and your mind is clear

Do not resist and do not cling
To worry, doubt, or anything
That would disturb the inward flow
That brings you light and helps you grow

For fear and wanting will create
A prison you will come to hate
Release and let your spirit lead
And Source will meet your every need

102
HEAR THE MYSTERY
darrell scott

In the stillness there's a mystery
Where the deepest truths are abide
We will never know the answers
'Till we choose to look inside

And the voice that speaks the mystery
Uses language without sound
Through impressions of the spirit
Where such treasures do abound

Hear the whisper spoken gently
Like a fragile puff of wind
In a still, small voice it calls us
To a place where few have been

May we listen to the spirit
As we hear things yet untold
Yielding daily to the stillness
So the mystery will unfold

103
It's GREAT to RELATE
darrell scott

How wonderful this world would be
If wars and fighting all would cease
And we could live in harmony
And then embrace a lasting peace

There is a way out of this mess
If differences we put aside
And focus on relatedness
Which helps us to be unified

Much focus on diversity
Can cause division to arise
If focus is on unity
Too often we will compromise

Diversity we must respect
And always hope for unity
But if we learn how to connect
Oh! What a place our world could be!

So focus on how we relate
And everything will fall in place
Diversity we'll celebrate
And unity will show its face

104
JACKET
darrell scott

I remember plays and parties
Gentle kisses, graceful dancing
Windswept beaches, moonlight pathways
Clubhouse dinners and romancing

Feeling heartbeats and embraces
Clothed with fragile youthful pride
But with time, as beauty faded
I was slowly cast aside

Soon forgotten, left forsaken
Tucked away and see no more
Worn and wrinkled, I'm now hanging
In your local Goodwill Store

105
LENNY GOT IT RIGHT
darrell scott

The first time that I caught her gaze
I wasn't that impressed
While others were intrigued by her
I wasn't - - - I confess

But once again I saw her
And my admiration grew
I saw the mystery in her eyes
And suddenly I knew

Why everyone adores her
Even if it takes a while
'Cause each of us were captured
By the shadow of her smile

Some paintings we remember
Some fade into the night
But Lisa will remain with us
'Cause Lenny got it right!

106
LIFE'S GOALS
darrell scott

Each New Year's Eve new goals I set
But by the end of March I knew
That not one goal was fully met
I never seemed to follow through

Until a wise and noble friend
Revealed a better way to live
She taught me how to comprehend
The gifts that life would love to give

My worry ceased and I would find
Her wisdom helped me come to see
That my ambitions kept me blind
From seeing goals life had for me

And as I yielded to life's flow
Awareness brought me such release
Now purpose takes me where I go
And I am filled with inner peace

Stop setting goals and be aware
In all that you desire to do
That Source will always gladly share
Those plans and goals life has for you!

107
R.I.P.
darrell scott

We see the words on marble stone
Three words for those who are deceased
Advice to those who now are gone
Three words of comfort: "Rest in Peace"

For most cannot attain that goal
Their anxious thoughts have kept them bound
While outer things consume their soul
Until they're buried in the ground

But listen to that inner voice
With healing words it wants to give
That urges us to make a choice
To "rest in peace" while we yet live!

108
TWO TREES

Two trees both grow within your heart
The choice you make is up to you
One makes you wise, one makes you smart
They give you different points of view

The tree of good - - and evil, too
Will soon produce a frenzied mind
While all the while you will pursue
Elusive peace you'll never find

The tree of life makes you aware
Of every moment that you live
Your heart of joy will want to share
With others you will freely give

Our thoughts imprison us - - 'tis sad
As Shakespeare wrote so long ago
"There is no good – there is no bad
But only thinking makes it so"!

109
HIGHER DESIRE
darrell scott

Michael David went to church
When he was only seven
The preacher spoke of Disneyland
Except he called it, "Heaven"

He told about those golden streets
With mansions all a-glitter
The parks are green – It's quite a scene
There isn't any litter

So Mike said, "Let's just go there, Dad
Instead of Disneyland!"
His Father sighed, and then replied
"You just don't understand!"

"You can't go there by car or train
Or even if you fly
For you to get to Heaven, son
You first would have to die!"

So Michael thought a minute
Then he slowly shrugged his shoulder
He said, "You know, I'd like to go
But only when I'm older!"

110
MOBSTER LOBSTER
darrell scott

I ordered a lobster last time I ate out
I was hungry for seafood that night
The waiter brought one that had broken a claw
"He broke it", he said, "In a fight"

That really upset me – and I told him so
"I do want a lobster for dinner
But why bring me this one?" I angrily asked
"Go back there and bring me the winner!"

OTHER BOOKS BY DARRELL SCOTT
www.dscottbooks.com

 Darrell Scott has authored, or co-authored 15 published books, including the best-seller, *Rachel's Tears*, the story of his daughter Rachel, the first victim of the Columbine high school shootings.

Darrell and his wife Sandy started a non-profit organization called, *Rachel's Challenge*, in Rachel's memory. Through its 50 presenters, Rachel's Challenge has reached over 28 million people in live settings over the last 18 years.

Rachel's Challenge has won 3 Emmy Awards through its television partners. They partner with Chuck and Gena Norris by providing character programming for the Norris's "KickStart Kids" organization. They also partner with the Cal Ripken, Sr. Foundation as well as with Marzano Research, one of the most prestigious K-12 research firms in the nation.

Darrell has appeared on numerous television programs such as Oprah, Larry King Live, Good Morning America, Dateline, O'Reilly Factor, Anderson Cooper, etc. He has been featured on the cover of Time magazine and quoted in Newsweek, the Wall Street Journal, and many other publications.

Darrell does keynote addresses for leadership teams of such organizations as Southwest Airlines, Bank of America, Sprint, BNSF Railroad, Motorola, and many others. He has met with Presidents Clinton, Bush, and Trump several times.

Darrell and his wife, Sandy, live in Lone Tree, Colorado where they enjoy their children and grandchildren.

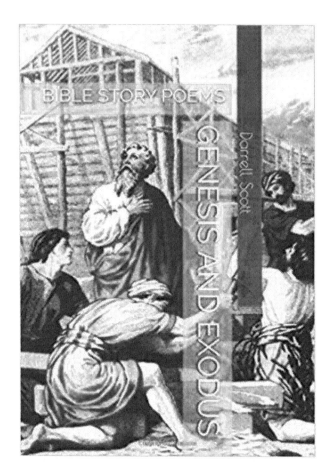

This is the first in the series on Bible Story Poetry. It features poems on all the Bible stories in Genesis and Exodus.

This is not your typical Bible Story Book for small children. This is for teens and adults and provides an entertaining and humorous, fresh approach to Bible reading.

A great source for pastors and youth pastors from which to illustrate their lessons or sermons.

Titles such as: When God Split sn Adam, Raisin' Cain,
Huge Dudes, Boat Man, The Drunk and the Punk, Stranger Danger,
Babblin' in Babel, Salty Lady, Expensive Soup, Wrestlemania, and
many more!

One example:

RAISIN' CAIN

Now Adam and Eve had a son they named Cain
Who worked in the field with the corn and the grain
They then had another boy - they named him Abel
He worked with the sheep and kept meat on the table

Now God had rejected an offering from Cain
But Abel's was blessed and it drove Cain insane
His anger was raging and soon he would kill
His young brother Abel while out in the field

Now Cain was in trouble and soon it got deeper
He said to the Lord "Am I my brother's keeper?"
Then God spoke to Cain and said, "I'll bring you down
Your poor brother's blood has cried out from the ground"

"I'll send you away from your family and home
And all through the earth you will wander and roam"
Then Cain said to God, "You are surely aware
My punishment, Lord, is just too hard to bear"

Cain reaped what he sowed when he disobeyed God
He soon had to leave for a place that's called 'Nod'
Poor Adam and Eve - they were nearly insane
Cause now they'd lost Abel and couldn't raise Cain

BIBLE VERSES
Genesis 4:1-15   Hebrews 11:4

www.dscottbooks.com

145

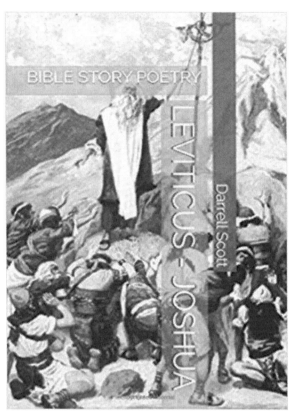

This is the second in the series on Bible Story Poetry. It features poems on all the Bible stories in Leviticus, Numbers, Deuteronomy, and Judges.

This is not your typical Bible Story Book for small children. This is for teens and adults and provides an entertaining and humorous, fresh approach to Bible reading.

A great source for pastors and youth pastors from which to illustrate their lessons or sermons.

Titles such as: Naughty Boys, Don't Get Stoned, Nose Vomit, Wise Spies and Gutless Guys, Nutty Staff, Mission Unaccomplished, Family Feud, Israelite Snake Bite, The Ass with Class, Bellyache Mistake, Nun Fun, Ouch, and many more.

www.dscottbooks.com

Example: **NOSE VOMIT**

The Israelites complained about the food they had to eat
'Cause manna was their daily meal and they were craving meat
So Moses was disgusted and he let Jehovah know
"These dummies you have given me have caused a lot of woe"

"I'm sick of all these people, they all act like I'm their father
Why did you save these idiots? Why did you even bother?"
"They grumbled from the day we left - they built a golden cow
I'm sick and tired of leading them, so please – just kill me now"

I'm not exaggerating, that is really what he said
His cup was full from all their bull, he'd just as soon be dead
The God spoke back to Moses and he said, "I've heard their plea
If they are tired of manna, then I'll give a guarantee

For one full month I'll feed them quail 'til it runs out their nose
The meat will stick between their teeth and some will decompose
And sure enough he sent the quail - it was a clever trick
For weeks that's all they had to eat and most of them got sick

And just as God predicted quail was dripping through their snout
Their sinus drainage was a mess - they couldn't blow it out
And some got stuck between their teeth where it would putrefy
And if you smelled their stinky breath, you'd probably want to die

God sent his fire and many died - a lesson would be learned
Be careful what you ask for if the answer gets you burned

BIBLE VERSES
Numbers 11

www.dscottbooks.com

The TRANSFORMATION of KENT CLARKSON
Becoming a Spiritual Superman

Darrell Scott

Follow the story of Kent Clarkson, mild-mannered youth pastor, and his wife, Louise on a journey from frustration to fulfillment.

Full of spiritual principles that take us beyond religious ritual into spiritual reality.

Sample: You see, for you and I to live the Christian life is not hard - - - it's totally impossible! But until we finally learn that lesson, and realize that we can't - - - we will continue to try to "please God" and "work for Him". As you will see in the coming pages, that was never what God intended for us.

What Kent didn't know, was that his life was about to change forever. The next few years would take him to places in God he never really dreamed were possible. He would be transformed from a mild-mannered youth pastor, to an unshakeable "Superman" in God's kingdom. He was about to learn that God's ways were completely different from Kent's ways.

www.dscottbooks.com

He was about to learn God's thoughts, and realize how wrong his had been. He didn't know it yet, but he was getting ready to learn how to fly!

Another sample: It is much easier to see our need to repent of sins at the first stage of our spiritual life than it is to see the need to repent of "dead works" after having been a Christian for several years. And yet, that is a necessary revelation before we are allowed to go to the next level of freedom in Christ!

Hebrews 6:1 talks about moving on to maturity in Christ. However, it tells us that we can't do this until we have laid a right foundation.

The first part of that foundation is "repentance from dead works"! These are foundations for Christians, not unbelievers. Unbelievers are convicted to repent of their sins, but here, believers are told that they must repent from 'dead works'.

Very few Christians understand the difference between repentance from sin and repentance from dead works, but there is a huge difference! Much of Kent's frustration came from the fact that he was not producing fruit, but was producing "dead works"!

His efforts were producing "wood, hay, and stubble" not "gold, silver, and precious stones". He had produced a lot of religious works, but very little spiritual fruit! He didn't even know that there was a difference!

Isaiah 50:4 (KJV) says: *"The Lord God hath given me the tongue of the learned, that I should know how to speak a word in season to him that is weary - -"*

This verse talks about having a "learned tongue" that enables a believer to: 1. Know how (developed skill) 2. To speak a word (not just any word, but the right word) 3. In season (the right time to speak the right word) 4. To him that is weary (not just to anyone, but to those ready to hear)

www.dscottbooks.com

149

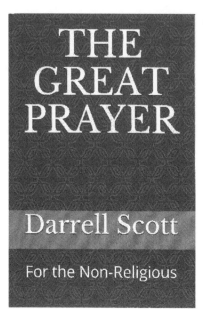

THE GREAT PRAYER

Darrell Scott

For the Non-Religious

This book is about the pattern given in the Lord's Prayer in a fresh and "out-of-the-box" approach. The prayer is broken down into 12 steps:

Prominence, Place, Praise, Participation, Provision, Pardon, Prevention, Protection, Possession, Power, Presence, and Permanence in Perspective.

It leads us to understanding of the harmony between meditation and prayer.

Sample: Prayer was never intended to be a self-serving communication tool to get what we want. Too often, prayer is viewed as a magical formula, like rubbing the bottle and hoping a genie appears to grant our wishes.

People will pray for a new car, a new home, a raise at work, or even to win the lottery. Sometimes that prayer is incorporated with a bribe, like, "God, if you will let me win the $40,000,000 lottery, I will give half of it to the poor and homeless." However, you can't trick the Creator by hiding greed beneath the façade of charitable generosity.

Too often prayer is ignored until a crisis arises. When a friend or family member gets sick, prayer is brought out of the closet to ask for their health or healing. This is far less selfish than asking to win the lottery, but it is still a very limited form of prayer, though a valid and understandable one. It boils down to a one way communication consisting of a request for relief.

www.dscottbooks.com

150

True prayer, as pointed out by Richard Rohr, requires us to take off our *calculating mind* and put on our *contemplative mind*. The calculating mind operates from the soul (psyche) and is self-centered. The contemplative mind operates from the spirit (pnuema) and is Source, or God-centered.

One of the vastly overlooked truths from scripture is the understanding of the separation of soul and spirit:
"For the word of God is living and active. Sharper than any double-edged sword, it penetrates even to dividing of soul and spirit" (Hebrews 4: 12 NIV).

The Bible teaches that we are transformed by the renewing of our minds (Rom. 12:2). It encourages us to let the same mind which was in Christ, be in us (Phil. 2:5). To be fleshly minded is death, but to be spiritually minded is life and peace (Rom 8:6).

The Divine Source of all of creation is not merely a vending machine whose sole function is to provide gifts whenever we plead for them. Mother Teresa said, *"Prayer is not asking. Prayer is putting oneself in the hands of God, at His disposition, and listening to His voice in the depth of our hearts."*

When "asking for things" is the essence of one's prayer, it reveals a level of spiritual immaturity.

We will take a closer look at the most quoted and well-known prayer of all: In Christian tradition it is called "The Lord's Prayer". It is short and simple, but full of content.

Jesus gave it to his disciples after they said to him, "Lord teach us to pray" (Luke 11:1). The instructions that he gave them, following that request, were not meant to be repeated as a mantra, but instead, to be a pattern for our interaction and communication with and from the Source of all life.

www.dscottbooks.com

151

LOSE YOUR MIND and FIND YOUR PURPOSE

The Path to Peace

Darrell Scott

Two respected spiritual leaders wrote the forward for this book: Dr. Mark Hanby and Bob Mumford.

This book engages a much needed subject that is too often ignored: The difference in your soul and spirit.

Sample: The goal of seeking is to find. But there are two extremely important things to understand before you start the search. #1 *What* am I seeking for, and #2 *Where* do I need to be seeking for it?

There are a multitude of "things" that people are seeking for. Eventually they find that "things" can never satisfy them. Wealth, fame, popularity, and power can never satisfy. Some of the most unhappy, miserable people on the planet are wealthy, powerful, and famous.

Even when you find the things you seek, those things are never enough. *"All I need is a little more"* becomes the eternal mantra. The reason people seek those things is because they think that "those things" will provide them with deep, lasting peace, incredible joy, and a sense of complete wholeness - - but they never will.

So really, what they are seeking for is not the "things", but the fulfillment, the peace, and the joy they believe those things can provide. But "things" will never produce lasting fulfilment, peace, and joy. The car, the boat, the house, etc. will quickly lose its initial appeal and become just another "thing" that we own. Even the best relationships cannot bring permanent peace, joy, and fulfillment.

Once you have learned that "things" can never bring you the fulfillment that you are seeking for, your search begins to go deeper - - below the surface.

www.dscottbooks.com

152

Many people never get to that deeper level of seeking. They spend their entire lives seeking it through material possessions, power, or fame.

Usually the deeper level of seeking will lead us to books, like this one, or mentors and teachers. So you read books, listen to teaching, and follow mentors, hoping that you will find answers from them. This is a good direction to take, but if you stop with the books, teachers, and mentors you will never arrive.

The books (including this one), mentors, and teachers can help tremendously by pointing the way to the ultimate answer within you. They are like arrows pointing you in the right direction - - but they cannot give you the treasure, because you already have it! They help remove the obstacles that have hidden the treasure from you.

The end goal is for you, individually, to find the treasure of righteousness, peace, and joy that has waited, within you, for you to discover. For we have this treasure in earthen vessels.

And that treasure has a Biblical name. It is called the Kingdom of God. The clearest definition of the Kingdom is found in Romans 14:17 (KJV): *"For the Kingdom of God is - - righteousness, peace, and joy - -"*.

The word "righteousness" can easily stop us in our tracks at this point. There are so many wrong beliefs and concepts about the word "righteousness", that I want to take a minute and help define it and then elaborate in a later chapter. "Righteousness" is not rules, regulations, doctrine, nor dogma.

It is simply an alignment of our soul with our spirit so that they are both in tune with God's purpose for our lives. The word has been so greatly distorted, that I will be using the word "alignment" instead of "righteousness" from this point on.

"Do I want ultimate fulfillment in my life? Do I want unspeakable joy and indescribable peace?

www.dscottbooks.com

153

"Truth is within ourselves. There is an inmost center in us all, where truth abides in fullness; and to know- - rather consists in opening out a way whence the imprisoned splendor may escape than in effecting entry for a light supposed to be without."

Robert Browning

Peace, joy, and fulfillment do not come from outward seeking, but from inward awareness. Light and truth are not objects to be reached for and retained, but rather, they are treasures within you that need to be recognized and released. This is what Robert Browning meant when he wrote about letting the imprisoned splendor escape instead of seeking to bring light into ourselves from without.

The great deception is that you must search for what you already have. This produces a never-ending quest to find the pot of gold at the end of the rainbow. As long as you are looking outside of yourself, the "gold" will never be found, because it doesn't exist "out there"!

In the movie, Raiders of the Lost Ark, there is a scene in which Indiana Jones realizes that people are looking for the Ark of the Covenant in the wrong place. They are working hard at finding something that they will never find because they are digging in the wrong location. And the reason they are digging in the wrong place is because they have faulty information. Their treasure map was inadequate, because they only had a part of the clue.

The goal of treasure hunting is to find out where the treasure is actually hidden. This is usually revealed through codes, keys, clues or maps designed to protect the treasure from anyone not possessing

www.dscottbooks.com

those aids. One missing piece of information on a treasure map, or one misleading clue and the treasure will never be found.

This book is designed to provide a treasure map of clues, keys, and codes that point toward the treasure. The words, poems, quotes, and commentaries are not the treasure - - they are simply clues that point toward the treasure.

You can memorize this book and all you will have done is memorize a map. The treasure will still be hidden until you follow the signs that lead to it.

Sometimes treasure hunting involves the process of elimination. This means that the first time you dig, you only discover that you are digging in the wrong place.

It may require rereading the treasure map several times, re-examining the clues, and continuing your search until you discover who you already are and the treasure you already own.

There is hidden treasure that every human heart longs to find. It is called different things, such as "happiness", "fulfillment", "purpose", "salvation", "nirvana", "redemption", "moksha", "enlightenment", and many other titles. Every person who has ever found that treasure knows that it is hidden within us and can never be found in any other location.

So - - if it really is that simple, why does the majority of the people continue to look for it through outside sources? What makes them believe that more money, fame, knowledge, or trinkets will make them happy, when there is ample proof that many of the most famous, wealthy people on earth are miserable?

The reason it seems difficult is because we live in a world of illusion guided by our senses and governed by our thoughts. We seek for answers in the outer realm of manifestation instead of the inner realm of source. The treasure maps we have believed all our lives have misled us into seeking the treasure "out there".

www.dscottbooks.com

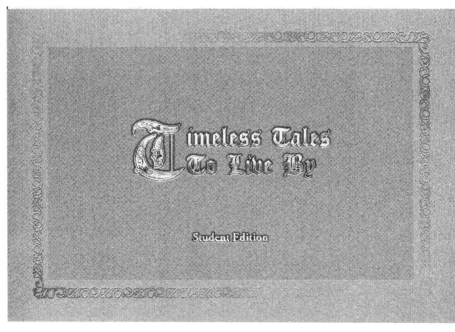

www.dscottbooks.com

This a remake of a number of Aesop's Fables in a book compiled by Darrell Scott and Jim May. It is full of life lessons for young people in the 10 – 14 age group. Comes also in a package with dvd for teacher or parent to use with illustrations. Below is a sample page

The Jar of Chocolate Drops

A boy came home from school hungry for a snack. He pulled a jar of chocolate drops down from the cabinet and thrust his hand into the jar to grab a big handful. When he clenched his fist around the chocolate, he could not get his hand through the narrow neck of the jar.

Though he tried and tried to pull his hand out, he would not let go of the candy. His wrist became sore and he started crying. His mother came in to see what was wrong. When she saw what he was trying to do she said, "Son, why don't you take out a smaller handful, and you can come back for more later. As long as you hold on to that many chocolate drops, you won't be able to get your hand out!"

MORAL
Sometimes we have to let go to be free.

How I can apply this story in my life: ....
....
....

www.dscottbooks.com

157

AWAKEN THE LEARNER

Finding the Source of Effective Education

Skills
Academic
Achievement
Collaboration
Critical Thinking
Communication   Creativity   Attitude

Hands
Head
Heart

Security   Identity   Belonging

Darrell Scott & Robert J. Marzano

www.dscottbooks.com

MOTIVATING & INSPIRING STUDENTS

S T U D E N T S

STRATEGIES TO AWAKEN THE LEARNER

Robert J. *Marzano*

Darrell *Scott*

Tina H. *Boogren*

Ming Lee *Newcomb*

Includes NEW Interviews

Foreword by Chuck & Gena Norris

Rachel's Tears

10 Years After Columbine...
Rachel Scott's Faith Lives On

Beth Nimmo and Darrell Scott
with Steve Rabey

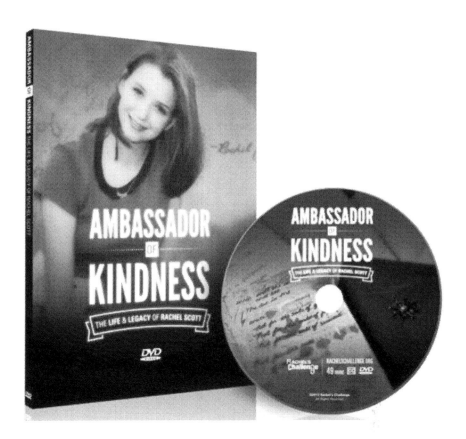

Rachel's story has been seen by millions of people through 5 television documentaries and a movie in theaters. 3 television Emmy Awards have been won because of her story.

This documentary is a powerful story about Rachel's life and legacy.

Rachel Scott, Columbine Victim,

Believed She Could

Change the World One Person at a Time

Chain

A Call to Compassionate Revolution

Reaction

DARRELL SCOTT

Coauthor of the Bestseller RACHEL'S TEARS

with STEVE RABEY

www.dscottbooks.com

Rachel Smiles

The Spiritual Legacy of Columbine Martyr Rachel Scott

*including powerful stories of
lives changed by one girl's faith*

DarrellScott
With Steve Rabey

www.dscottbooks.com

RACHEL AND ADAM

By: Darrell Scott
(Rachel's Dad)

180

CONNECTIONS

DAILY CONNECTIONS BETWEEN TEACHER AND STUDENTS

Mike Scott and Darrell Scott

Foreward by: Dr. Robert Marzano

Rachel's
Challenge

www.dscottbooks.com

Project: Teacher's Corner

Choose a corner of the room to create a display of your life so your students can better appreciate you as a person. Include pictures, from birth to the present. Also, put on display certificates, trophies, awards, etc. Feature pictures of yourself when you were your students' age.

The more they can see about you the better. If you played sports, were in the band, were on the debate team, choir, clubs, etc.

If you want to go to the trouble of setting up a video display through a television or monitor of home movies when you were a kid, then that would be icing on the cake!

1. **INFORMATION**: The saddest day of my life. Describe.

2. **ILLUSTRATION**: Share a picture, poem, or just the story.

3. **INTERACTION**: Share about the saddest day of your life.

   This one may seem morbid, but people draw closer together when they share about the deepest hurts in their lives versus their greatest triumphs.

   If you have rotated them into different groups each day, then by now they will have made several new friends or at least have gotten to know one another better.

www.dscottbooks.com

167

Made in the USA
Middletown, DE
05 April 2019